How to Start a Small Home Business

A Step By Step Guide to Starting a Successful Home Based Business

I0462829

By Meir Liraz

Published by BizMove
www.bizmove.com

Table of Contents

1. Essential Start-Up Strategies

If you're seriously considering working from home, you're not alone. Some 60 million Americans are currently doing so, compared with six million in 1984, according to the National Association of Home-Based Businesses. In five years, it is estimated that as many as one of every two workers will be engaged in a full- or part-time business or doing salaried work at home. For single parents and many women, this alternative facilitates juggling family and career. For fathers, it can lead to spending more time with their children. Working from home can provide the means for stretching a tight budget or finding a new career for those displaced by corporate downsizing. For the retired or the increasing number of people considering early retirement, it becomes a way of contributing, of staying alive and vibrant by not allowing their professional skills to atrophy. And for many with handicaps, it's the door to self-sufficiency and a productive future.

Choose Something You Enjoy and That People Will Pay For

Selecting an appropriate home-based business for yourself requires tuning in to the most popular radio station in the world: WPWPF ("What People Will Pay For"). And simple market research will help you do just that. Begin by asking prospective customers what they need. Go to trade shows and get feedback on your potential product or service. Find out who is in that business now and what advantages you might be able to offer over your competition.

If you are having trouble finding the ideal business, here are four possibilities:
* Turn what you most enjoy into a home-based venture, such as a favorite hobby or interest.

* Utilize existing skills from your salaried job.

* Solve a problem that people are willing to pay someone else to do for them.

* Use technology and resources you already have around the house, from your van to your computer.

Define Your Niche
It is much easier to market yourself as a specialist serving a particular niche. This helps you stand out from the competition, and also allows you to charge a decent fee because you are more than a general "worker" people can hire as an employee or from a

temp agency.

There are four primary ways to define your niche:
* WHO you serve -- e.g., a computer consultant who works only with women; a public relations firm that specializes in assisting environmentally-conscious companies; a caterer who handles parties and weddings for the Hungarian community.

* WHAT you provide -- e.g., a computer consultant who works only with Macs; a public relations firm that specializes in doing publicity book tours for authors; a caterer who prepares health food that looks and tastes decadent.

* WHERE you work -- e.g., a computer consultant who focuses on the east side of town; a public relations firm that specializes in getting media coverage in foreign countries; a caterer who has attained renown for servicing a variety of outdoor events.

* WHEN you are called upon -- e.g., a computer consultant who is available for weekend and after-hours calls; a public relations firm that specializes in crisis communications for companies involved in scandals or tragedies; a caterer who can be counted

on to handle even last-minute dinner parties with aplomb.

Charge What You Are Worth

The truth is that no one automatically knows what to charge; people generally have to discover what is both appropriate and competitive. Begin by doing some basic research to determine the following:

How much is your product or service worth in concrete terms? Value, like beauty, is in the mind of the beholder to a certain extent. There are several ways to ascertain the value of what you offer to prospective customers. Can someone currently obtain this product or service elsewhere? If so, how much are they paying for it?

What will people actually pay? Perception can be as important as the actual value of the product or service being offered. If potential customers perceive your price as being too high, you'll end up without a sale. By comparison, if buyers perceive something as being too cheap, they'll worry that it may be inferior in quality.

Above all, be careful not to sell yourself short.

Consider following this commonly-used pricing formula:

Direct Costs + Overhead + Profit = Your Price

* Direct costs refer to costs you incur in doing your job: gas, telephone calls, postage, printing and your time. Calculate your salary -- including fringe benefits -- into your rates. Remember to add enough to cover the hours of un-billable time you spend marketing and administering.

* Overhead refers to the general costs of doing business: equipment, software, utilities, office supplies, advertising and marketing expenses, and administrative costs. Most home businesses multiply their hourly wage by two or three to cover overhead.

* Profit is an amount calculated over and above direct and indirect expenses; many experts advise adding 15 to 20 percent or more.

2. Clever Marketing and Operational Strategies

Ideally, the space you select for your office will match your personal work style and budget, qualify you for tax benefits to which you're entitled, and fit in with your household environment. To work effectively at home, most people need these basic work areas:

* Space for a desk and chair, where you can work with a computer, phone and other frequently-used equipment.

* Conversation space with chairs or a couch where you can collect your thoughts or hold meetings.

* Storage space for filing cabinets, books and reference materials

* Shelf space for supplies and infrequently-used equipment.

* Large work space for activities such as assembling materials and doing mailings or shipping.

If you don't have a separate room that can be designated for your office, choose a location where you will be disturbed the least. For example, partition off a section of your living, family or dining room. Alternatively, convert or remodel a space such as your garage, attic, basement or porch.

Organize Your Work Space for Success

Keep those things you most frequently use near your desk, based on this simple formula. On a scale of one to seven, rate the item you're storing or filing in terms of how frequently you use it. Give items you use every day a one; those you use once a year, a seven. Place items in the following locations according to how you rate them:

* 1: Place all these items within arm's reach of your desk area.

* 2-3: Keep these items within your immediate range in files or cabinets, on countertops or on shelves.

* 4-5: Store these items in nearby cabinets or closets, or on shelves outside your office space.

* 6-7: Store these items in remote locations such as the attic, basement or garage.

Make Your Business Official and Visible

Many home-based businesses fall by the wayside because they do not make their operations official and visible. Consider the following actions to avoid that pitfall:

* Clarify any zoning restrictions on your running a business from home. Make sure you can operate a business from your residence and, if there are problems in doing so, get a separate mailing address or apply for a use permit or variance to your zoning laws.

* Open a business bank account. Keep your personal and business affairs distinct from one another.

* Get a separate phone line installed in your home for business calls. A separate line helps you manage your personal and business lives more easily, and gives you a more professional image.

* Maintain regular business hours. Nothing annoys customers more than not knowing when and if you are open for business.

* Select a memorable name that fits your business image. A dull, confusing or inappropriate name for

your business can result in clients overlooking you or not specifically understanding and appreciating what you have to offer them.

Create a Thoroughly Professional Image

A marginal business image leaves the impression that your home-based venture is not a truly professional one. So in setting up your enterprise, pay attention to key image components other than your business name that do not necessitate a big budget, but rather attention to detail. Here are some suggestions:

* Communicate quality with a custom-designed logo; avoid choosing one from a standard catalog.

* Apply this logo in a consistent way to give your company a professional and identifiable image on business cards, stationery, invoices, faxes and any other visual communications elements.

* Choose paper that looks and feels top quality for letterhead and business cards.

* Select professional locations for meetings with clients. If clients come to your home, avoid having them walk through personal or family areas, or

schedule meetings at outside sites such as restaurants or hotel lobbies.

Utilize Word-of-Mouth Marketing

Word-of-mouth marketing refers to two highly effective practices: networking and referrals.

Networking, the most popular way to start and build a home-based business, refers to using face-to-face contact to establish relationships that can generate leads. It's based on talking with people about what you do and listening carefully to find out how you might serve them. Consider joining a networking organization, often called a "leads club," which is set up specifically to generate business leads for members.

Once a business is established, word-of-mouth marketing means getting referrals from satisfied customers. Let your customers know you genuinely appreciate their referrals; by so doing, you multiply the number of mouths talking positively about what you have done or provided.

Make Sure People Can Reach You

Research shows that people working from home

spend more time talking on the telephone than on any other single activity. As a result, you need to be sure clients can always reach you so as not to jeopardize any business opportunities. Fortunately, a variety of sophisticated telephone equipment and services is available to ensure ongoing communication, as the following useful options demonstrate:

* Use voice mail to take messages when you're out of the office or unable to answer the telephone. Voice mail can be obtained from your phone company and other providers, or you can purchase an answering machine or add a voice mail system to your computer. Professional answering services and forwarding calls to the home of someone you hire are more expensive solutions.

* Use call forwarding to receive calls when you're out of the office. Other alternatives include purchasing a cellular phone, a 700 number or a pager.

* To handle incoming calls while you're on the telephone, get call waiting or voice mail that picks them up so people never get a busy signal.

* To prevent unnecessary interruptions, subscribe to your local phone company's VIP alert so only desired calls come through during the time periods you designate.

* if you are running short of phone lines, get distinctive ringing that gives you two phone numbers on one line, or double up on one line by purchasing a combination fax/phone/answering machine that automatically recognizes when a fax is coming through.

3. How to Deal with the IRS and Formal Business Requirements

Operating a home business on a full- or part-time basis may require taking certain legal steps to protect yourself and your venture, including the following:

* Get an employer's ID number if you have employees or are incorporated or in a partnership.

* Obtain a federal license if your job is covered by federal laws, such as those who are investment advisors or firearms dealers; similarly, make sure you have any required state and local business licenses.

* Obtain the trademarks, copyrights or patents needed to protect any products or services you have created.

* Incorporate or form a limited-liability company or a partnership if you are not a sole proprietor and are working with other people.

* Find out if you are required to collect sales tax for your product or service. If so, register with the state agency responsible for collecting sales taxes.

* Register your business name if you are using a name other than your own or a variation thereof.

Consult a lawyer or the appropriate government agencies in your city and state if you're not sure how these requirements may apply to your business or locale.

Claim Your Deductions

Whether you live and work in a house, apartment or condominium, you can deduct the cost of operating and maintaining that part of your residence used for business if you meet the basic criteria established by the IRS for a home office.

According to the IRS, the portion of your home you wish to claim as a tax write-off must be used exclusively and regularly for business.

In addition, the portion of your home you use must be either your principal place of business or a location where you meet with customers or clients in the normal course of business activities.

If you qualify for a home-office deduction, you can deduct a variety of expenses such as your mortgage payments and capital improvements, pro rated for the portion of your residence used as an office.

As a self-employed individual, you can also deduct numerous ordinary business expenses, from the cost of operating your car to dues you pay to professional and trade associations. However, be sure the IRS considers you a self-employed individual or independent contractor rather than an employee. The rules on this issue and on expense deductions can be tricky, so it's wise to consult your accountant for clarification.

Get Needed Insurance
Many home-based firms don't realize that their homeowner's or apartment dweller's insurance may not protect them against three basic business contingencies:

* Home/apartment insurance usually doesn't cover business property. Consider purchasing business property insurance to cover your computer and other office equipment and furnishings.

* Home/apartment insurance usually doesn't cover liability for accidents or injuries to customers or

business visitors. Consider purchasing a rider to your policy to cover anyone who comes to your home on business.

* Standard auto insurance usually doesn't cover damaged or stolen business property. If you use your car for business, be sure to indicate that on your policy and pay the additional amount required.

Finally, depending on the nature of your business and the level of risk you want to assume, you may also wish to purchase any of the following:

* Malpractice or errors or omissions (E&O) insurance to cover you against claims that your product or service harmed someone or caused a business loss.

* Disability insurance to cover you against loss of income should you become disabled.

* Partnership insurance to cover you against suits arising from the actions of any partners you have.

4. Essential Financial Management Strategies

Depending on the nature of your business, it can take from six months to a year to get underway, one to three years to turn a profit, and three to five years to become self-sustaining. This means you must have enough money to cover your costs of living and doing business during this start-up period. Consider these five entry plans as options:

* The Moonlighting Plan. Keep your full-time job and develop your business as a sideline until it takes off and you can rely on it entirely for your livelihood.

* The Part-time Plan. Work a part-time job to provide a base income while you're building up the operation.

* The Spin-off Plan. Turn your previous employer into your first major customer or, if ethically possible, take a major client from your previous job to help launch your fledgling venture.

* The Piggyback Plan. If you have a working spouse or partner, reduce expenses so you can live on one salary until your business gets underway.

* The Have-Your-Clients-Finance-You Plan. If you have sufficient stature or expertise in your field, obtain retainer contracts with a few clients for one year so you will have an assured source of revenue.

Arrange for Start-up Funds

Fortunately, most home businesses do not involve extensive start-up costs. As a result, most people can "bootstrap" their fledgling operation using money from the following sources:

* Credit cards. You can put many business expenses on a credit card. However, try to limit charges to items that will pay for themselves by generating income relatively quickly.

* Personal loans. If you or a spouse has an existing job and a good credit record, banks will usually give you a personal loan more readily than a business loan.

* Home equity loans. If you own your home, refinancing it is one way to obtain a reservoir of start-up capital.

* Character-based microloans. The U.S. Small Business Administration and a variety of private

foundations offer microloan programs for very small businesses to handle loans ranging from less than $1000 to $25,000. These loans are not based on a person's assets but rather on good character and proven management ability.

Get Written Agreements

When you work from home, contracts are your most important safeguard against problems with customers and clients, and help ensure that you are taken seriously as a business. Whatever your endeavor, create a standard contract to use, spelling out specifics such as what you will provide, when you will provide it, what it will cost, and when customers or clients are obliged to pay you.

While contracts can be verbal or written, written ones are certainly preferable. The best way to develop contract agreements that are customized to your specific needs is to consult an attorney. You can also talk with colleagues about the contracts they use, ask your professional or trade association for information, or attend a workshop on contracting. Many pro forma contracts are also available on computer software.

Keep Cash Flowing

If you are self-employed, having a system for managing your cash flow is essential to the survival of your business. To use an analogy, cash flow is to your livelihood what breath is to life. The following seven steps will help ensure that the money you're owed comes in as quickly as possible:

* Get deposits, retainers or partial progress payments as often as you can.

* Get payment up front for expenses or arrange to charge them to your client's account.

* Bill immediately upon delivery of a service or product, instead of waiting until the end of the month.

* Take bank cards instead of extending credit.

* Use a check guarantee service so you can accept checks safely.

* Offer discounts of two to five percent for receipt of payment within 20 days from the date of invoicing.

* Act promptly on overdue accounts. The longer the account is overdue, the less likely it is to be paid.

5. Home Business Time Management Strategies

It's tempting to sleep late or spend extra time reading the newspaper when you work from home. But since you're your own boss, you need to get started promptly and keep working on a regular schedule. Here are several suggestions:

* Take action. Sit down at your desk, make up or review a "to do" list, and then begin with the most interesting task on the list.

* Set a deadline for yourself to complete a given project by a certain time.

* Bribe yourself by promising a reward if you accomplish a specific task.

Once you get started, your work can develop a momentum that keeps you going all day. We've also found, however, that taking a break every few hours contributes to an increase in productivity and creativity.

Set Specific Boundaries
Even the most carefully constructed plans are

vulnerable to interruptions and distractions. The most common ones you are likely to encounter fall into these three categories:

* Household responsibilities. Don't let errands and household activities become a regular part of your workday. Cultivate the attitude that even though you are physically at home, you are mentally at work.

* Family and friends. Talking to your spouse, children or friends can potentially consume much of your time. Instead, work out a clear plan with your loved ones and get their support. Let them know when you will be working so they will avoid disturbing your concentration.

* Losing focus. Don't interrupt yourself with office minutia or extraneous phone calls. Set up your environment to help you stay focused on the job at hand. Put temptation out of sight as much as possible.

If disruptions continue to be the bane of your workday, consider relocating your office to a different area of the house or changing your office hours, perhaps working after the children are asleep or early in the morning before other activities have started.

Make Time for Your Private Life

As your own boss, it's also easy to become a workaholic and inadvertently neglect your personal life, family and fun. Follow these recommendations to avoid burnout and depression from undertaking too much work:

* Set up a firm schedule. Establish a fixed stopping point every day and do not compromise on this except for emergencies. If needed, develop a closing ritual such as a walk around the block or taking a class to make sure you get out of the office at a set time.

* Protect your free time. Make sure clients know your work hours, and do not take calls or allow business visitors to "drop by" at any hour.

* Establish minibreaks. Set aside five to 15 minutes a day to "do nothing." Spend that time doing something you enjoy such as gardening, playing with a pet, or sitting in the sun.

If you tend to overwork, it is crucial to develop new

values that support a healthier and more balanced, productive and secure life. Never underestimate the therapeutic effects of relaxing on a regular basis.

Use Technology to Streamline Your Operations
Home-office technology can streamline many of your most time-consuming administrative tasks -- and save you money. Here are a few examples:

* Use the templates that come with your word processor for standardized documents such as fax cover sheets and invoices.

* Learn to rely on the spell checker, grammar checker, dictionary and electronic thesaurus features that are part of many software packages to enhance the accuracy and quality of your business documents.

* Scan names, addresses and phone numbers directly from business cards into your computer using a card scanner.

* Use special preprinted papers from companies like Paper Direct (800/APAPERS) and Queblo (800/523-9080) to produce attractive customized flyers, business cards, presentation folders,

brochures and newsletters quickly.

In addition, many kinds of technologically-advanced equipment are available that enable you to speed up daily tasks. These include programmable telephones, high-speed printers, electronic postage scales, electric staplers, letter-opening machines, letter folders and dictation equipment.

6. How to Make Your Work More Satisfying and Rewarding

We believe success is always a joint venture. You can't do it alone -- and you don't need to. Seeking out help when you require it is basic to success whatever you undertake professionally. In fact, research shows that those who are most successful on their own are willing to pay for needed information and expertise. They also hire experts to help them carry out aspects of their business they know little about or are too busy to handle.

Here are a few guidelines that show when you can actually save money by bringing in outside assistance:

* When the time you could spend on business matters exceeds the cost of the hired help. An example would be hiring a computer consultant to solve your hardware problems so you can take on an extra project.

* When the cost of hiring someone is self-liquidating. An example would be paying someone to produce a newsletter that generates more business for you.

* When you have more to lose through lack of knowledge than the cost of someone else's expertise. An example would be hiring a public relations specialist to obtain publicity for you rather than trying to do so yourself if you have no experience in this field.

Keep in Contact

To avoid feeling isolated, working from home requires you to take the initiative and become involved in the world around you. Here are seven ways to keep in contact with peers and colleagues:

* Join community organizations and professional, technical or trade associations.

* Read specialty publications such as newsletters, professional and trade journals, and magazines to keep you informed about what's happening in your field.

* Attend relevant workshops, seminars and courses.

* Take an electronic coffee break using your computer and an on-line service.

* Schedule regular breakfast, lunch or dinner meetings with peers.

* Set up or join a networking group that meets on a regular basis.

* Affiliate or form joint business relationships, or start a partnership.

Whichever options you choose, don't neglect the importance of personal and professional friendships.

Choose Rewarding Work

One of the best things about self-employment is that you can tailor your work to fit your own values, priorities and lifestyle. If you want to put your family first, for example, you can select work hours and a vocation that let you devote more time to them. If you want to pursue artistic endeavors, you can pick a career that enables you to utilize your creativity. The key is finding a match between what you desire from life and what the world needs and will pay for.

The message here is to clearly define your goal and determine how you can utilize your skills to achieve that goal. As you will see, the most amazing thing about being self-employed is that the more closely the work you do fits who you are, who you want to become and how you want to live, the more successful you'll be.

7. Things You Must Consider Before You Start

What's the perfect home business for you? You've listed your skills. You've outlined your interests. You've described your family's preferred lifestyle. You've come up with a business idea. Next, consider such questions as: Are there customers for my product or service? How do I know? How will I find them? Who are my competitors? What will I charge? How will I promote my product or service? Finding the answers to these questions is the challenging and sometimes tedious homework that will help you determine your chances for success, and whether you should look for another more marketable idea.

What Is My Product?

"I bathe and groom poodles and small dogs." "I design, construct, and sell roll-top desks." "I provide accounting services to small business clients."

"I make dried flower arrangements." "I teach intermediate and advanced piano to children." "I design and implement direct mail advertising campaigns for small businesses and nonprofit organizations."

The first step in creating a business is to decide what your product is. What are you selling? Practice writing a short, specific statement describing your product or service. Getting a clear idea of a business concept is one of the most difficult tasks in creating a business. Your statement may change several times as you experiment with the market and test your skills. Instead of "I make toys," you may want to narrow your product line to "I make wooden dolls." Instead of "I write software programs for small business needs," you may decide to tap into a big market and "provide training for employees of small businesses in the use of accounting packages." See how it feels to describe your product or service to family, friends, potential customers, and fellow business people. Is your description clear and brief? Can you say it with confidence and enthusiasm?

Who Will Buy It?

To develop and test your business idea, answer the question "Who will buy my product or service?" Make a list of potential customers: individuals, groups, segments of the population, or other businesses that need your product or service. If you are making fabric-covered lap boards for people confined to bed, how will you quickly and inexpensively find a market?
Through hospitals or home nursing care organizations? Through craft stores by displaying them as gift items? In mail order catalogues? Is there a market avenue that will reach children? Ask friends and colleagues for help in brainstorming all

the possible markets (customers) and uses for your product or service.

Who Is the Competition?

Your business planning must also include an up-to-date analysis of your competition. Why? Because you need to plan your market position--how you will fit into the marketplace. Will your product or service be cheaper or more expensive than that of the major competitions? Will it be more durable? Will you be open during hours that your competitors are closed? What benefits can you build into your product or service that your competitors don't offer? Will you do rush jobs?

In planning your business, look for a unique niche that will give you freedom from strong competition or that will make your product or service more valuable than others in the market. If you plan to open a day-care center and find that none in your area is open before school, early opening might make your service more competitive. If you discover that local caterers have overlooked the office party market, you might highlight that in your brochure. The more you can learn about your competition, the better you'll be able to decide how to position yourself in the market.

Newspaper ads and trade magazines are other good

sources of market information. Check also with the Chamber of Commerce, your county office of economic development, the Census Bureau, and business and professional organizations to gather market and pricing data.

Where Are the Buyers? How Can I Find Them?
As you become more familiar with the competition, you will also be discovering where and how to find buyers. Whatever the type of home business you want to open, you will need to do market research to determine if there are buyers for your idea, where they are, and how to find them. (And in the process, you will also be gathering information on pricing.)

Search the Internet and visit your local library to compile local and county statistics on the size and makeup of your market. (While you are at the library, check out some books on marketing research so you will know what you are getting into.) Also, check those of the following resources that might have data about your product or service or the people who would use it:

Encyclopedia of Associates. Gale Research Company, Book Tower, Detroit, MI 48226.

Ayer Directory of Publications. Lists trade

publications by subject matter. Contact the sales, marketing, or research departments for buying patterns among their readers.

"Survey of Buying Power." Sales, Marketing, Management Magazine. July issue each year.

Thomas' Register. Lists companies by product and service line, organized geographically and alphabetically.

Directory of Business, Trade, and Public Policy Organizations. U.S. Small Business Administration, Office of Advocacy.

Department of Commerce Publications. Data User Series Division, Bureau of the Census, Washington, D.C. 20233.

County Business Patterns. U.S. Department of Commerce, Bureau of the Census. Available for each state.

When your marketing research is completed you will have 1) identified your potential customers; 2) found out all you can about their habits, needs, preferences, and buying cycles; and 3) decided how to reach them to generate sales.

How Much Shall I Charge?

Four main factors will help you decide what to charge for your product or service: 1) your direct and indirect costs; 2) the profit you want to make; 3) your market research data on competitors' prices; and 4) the urgency of the market demand. There is rarely an exact "right" price but rather an acceptable price range within which you will want to fall. Avoid the common mistakes made by many new business owners--charging too much or too little. Use several approaches to arrive at a cost and "test" the price. If your ego is too involved, your price may be too high. On the other hand, if you have the attitude that "this is just a little something I do in my spare time" or "anybody could do this," then your price may be too low.

Here is a formula for setting a fair price. Calculate your price using other approaches, too, before you make a final decision on price:

Typical Pricing Formula
1. Direct Material Costs--Figure the total cost of the raw materials you have to use to make up your item. Figure the cost of a group of items and then divide by the number of items to find the cost per item. If you can easily and immediately determine the material cost of a single item, fine. Some items are produced in batches, however, and it is easier to get an item cost by dividing the cost of a batch by the

number of items eventually produced.

2. Direct Labor Costs--Figure what you pay to employees to produce the item (whether or not you have employees now). You must assign a wage figure, even if you are the only one producing the item. Take the weekly salary you pay someone to produce the necessary number of items and divide it by the number of items. Add this figure to the Direct Material Costs total.

Materials + Labor = $_____.

3. Overhead Expenses--These expenses include rent, gas and electricity, business telephone calls, packing and shipping supplies, delivery and freight charges, cleaning, insurance, office supplies, postage, payroll taxes, repairs, and maintenance. The accuracy of your costing depends on estimating logical amounts for all categories of expenses. If you are working at home, figure a portion of your total rent or mortgage payment (in proportion to your work space and storage areas), or assign a reasonable, competitive rent figure for the same amount and type of space. List all overhead expense items and total them. Divide the total overhead figure by the number of items per month (or time period you used above). The answer is your overhead per item

Overhead + Materials + Labor = Total Cost/Item

4. Profit--Include an amount added to the cost of each item so you won't end up just breaking even or making the employees' wages. Check your competition and see what they are charging. (Retailers generally double the wholesale price.) If your product is a little better than the competition, charge a little more. If your product is comparable, price it similarly. Remember, you will get the profit from each sale, in addition to the salary figure. Add the profit figure you have chosen to the total cost per item to get your total price per item.

Profit + Total Cost/Item = Total Price/Item

Remember, the main purpose in operating a business is to make a profit. Don't undersell your product or service just because "I'd be baking cakes anyway" or "I'm just starting out" or" I work out of my home." If you have a new, rare, handmade product or personalized service, the demand may be so high that customers are willing to pay a little more.

Promotion
Promotion is an overall, long-range plan designed to inform potential customers about what you have

to sell. Advertising is usually thought of as the paid communication part of the promotion program.

To develop a total promotional campaign you must answer these questions: 1) What image or message do I want to promote? 2) What are the best media and activities for reaching my potential customers? 3) How much time and money can I spend on the effort?

Develop a long-range, consistent program for building image and reaching customers. Your image should be reflected in your business card, logo, stationery, brochure, newsletter, telephone answering service, signs, paid ads, and promotional activities.

Word-of-mouth recommendations from satisfied customers are the very best promotion any business can have. Consider which promotional tactics will build the confidence and image you are looking for--giving speeches and interviews (often good for counselors, teachers, lawyers, consultants), having an open house or holiday home sale (for craftspeople), holiday recitals or shows (for music and dance teachers or day-care operators), free demonstrations and samples (for retailers, decorators, caterers).

Several small ads may have more impact than one large, splashy ad. Conduct a campaign rather than having a one-shot ad or event. If you hire a public relations firm, look for one that can give you personal attention and develop a total marketing plan for you, not just a couple of ads. The plan should include market research, a profile of your target audience, a clear description of the image they recommend you project, the written copy, and a list of media (including cost and scheduling calendars) that are best for your type of product or service. As a new small business owner, you will probably decide to set aside a certain dollar amount per year or a percentage of past, current, or projected sales for paid advertising.

You're The Boss

A telling sign on a new business owner's desk read: "Yesterday I didn't even know how to spell ENTREPRENEUR and now I am one!" Now that you have decided to open a home-based business, all decisions will be your responsibility, not just those you previously enjoyed because they involved your area of expertise. Of course, as a day-care operator you already knew how to soothe an upset child, but as the owner of that business, do you know when to file your taxes? As a consultant you have over 20 years' experience advising organizations on personnel matters, but do you know if it's to your advantage to incorporate? You are an expert at word processing, but do you know how to develop an efficient record keeping and billing system? You are the boss now and the good health of your business depends on your management skills.

8. Complete Step by Step Starting Guide

Homework has taken on new meaning recently. The drive for economic self-sufficiency has motivated large numbers of persons to market their skills and talents for profit from home. Our increasingly service oriented economy offers a widening spectrum of opportunities for customized and personalized small business growth.

Though untrained entrepreneurs have traditionally had a high rate of failure, small businesses can be profitable. Success in small home based business is not an accident. It requires both skills in a service or product area and acquisition of management and attitudinal competencies.

The purpose of this guide is to help you take stock of your interests, aptitudes and skills. Many people have good business ideas but not everyone has what it takes to succeed. If you are convinced that a profitable home business is attainable, this guide will provide step by step guidance in development of the basic written business plan.

Information Gathering

While the reasons for the rapid growth of home

based business operations may vary from the need to supplement family income with few hundred dollars all the way to a sophisticated technical consulting service billing hundreds of thousands of dollars, there are many common characteristics and challenges to be considered in launching most home based businesses, regardless of size. Some tasks are universal to all small business startups, while others are unique to a home base.

Careful planning, based on interviews with dozens of home based operators over the past decade indicate that special planning is required to research legal and tax issues, proper space utilization and to establish time management discipline. Inadequate or careless attention to development of a detailed business plan can be costly for you and your family in terms of lost time, wasted talent and disappearing dollars.

The Entrepreneurial Personality

A variety of experts have documented research that indicates that successful small business entrepreneurs, whether male or female, have some common characteristics. How do you measure up? On this checklist, write a "Y" if you believe the statement describes you; an "N" if it doesn't; and a "U" if you can't decide:

_____ I have a strong desire to be my own boss.

_____ Win, lose or draw, I want to be master of my own financial destiny

_____ I have significant specialized business ability based on both my education and my experience.

_____ I have an ability to conceptualize the whole of a business; not just its individual parts, but how they relate to each other

_____ I develop an inherent sense of what is "right" for a business and have the courage to pursue it.

_____ One or both of my parents were entrepreneurs; calculated risk-taking runs in the family

_____ My life is characterized by a willingness and capacity to persevere.

_____ I possess a high level of energy, sustainable over long hours to make the business successful.

While not every successful home based business

owner starts with a "Y" answer to all of these questions, three or four "N"'s and "U"'s should be sufficient reason for you to stop and give second thought to going it alone. Many proprietors who sense entrepreneurial deficiencies seek extra training and support their limitations with help from a skilled team of business advisors such as accountants, bankers and attorneys.

Selecting a Business

Perhaps you have already decided what your home based business will be. You know how you will serve your market and with what. If not, but you are determined to establish a home based source of income, then you need to decide exactly what business you will enter. A logical first step for the undecided is to list potential areas of personal background, special training, educational and job experience, and special interests that could be developed into a business.

Time Management

For both the novice and the experienced business person planning a small home based enterprise, an early concern requiring self-evaluation is Time Management.

It is very difficult for some people to make and keep work schedules even in the disciplined setting of an employer's office. At home, as your own boss, the problem can be much greater To determine how much time you can devote to your business, begin by drafting a weekly task timetable listing all current and potential responsibilities and the blocks of time required for each. When and how can business responsibilities be added without undue physical or mental stress on you and your family? Potential conflicts must be faced and resolved at the outset and as they occur Otherwise, your business can become a nightmare. During the first year of operation, continue to chart, post and check off tasks on a daily weekly, monthly basis. Distractions and excuses for procrastination abound. It is important to keep both a planning and an operating log. These tools will help avoid oversights and provide vital information when memory fails. To improve the quality of home work time, consider installation of a separate telephone line for the business and attach an answering machine to take messages when you do not wish to be distracted or are away from home. A business line has the added advantage of allowing you to have a business listing in the phone book and, if you wish to buy it, an ad in the classified directory

Is a Home Based Business Site Workable?

Where in the home will the business be located?

What adjustments to living arrangements will be required?

What will be the cost of changes?

How will your family react?

What will the neighbors think?

It will be important to set aside a specific work area. For example, more than one fledgling business ledger has gone up in smoke, been chewed by the family dog, or thrown out with the trash when business records were not kept separate from family papers. Ready access to business records during work hours is essential, but they must be protected.

Check the reasons below for and against working at home that apply to you. List any additional drawbacks or obstacles to operating this business at home.

Pros / Cons

Lower startup costs / Isolation

Lower fixed costs / Space limitations

Tax benefits / Zoning

Lifestyle flexibility / Security concerns

No commuting / Household

_____ / interference

_____ _____

_____ _____

Note that changes in personal habits will be required. Examples:

Self discipline to keep TV off while working.

Limiting personal telephone calls in length and number

Diligence in meeting work deadlines when no one is checking

Ask family members to comment on pros and cons. Their concerns may require reconsideration of some specifics.

Is a Home Based Business Site Allowable?

Now you will want to investigate potential legal and

community problems associated with operating the business from home. You should gather read and digest specialized information concerning laws and regulations concerning home based business operations.

Check first! Get the facts in writing. Keep a topical file for future reference. Some facts and forms will be needed for your business plan. There may be limitations enforced that can make your planned business impossible or require expensive modifications to your property

Items to be investigated, recorded and studied are:

County or city zoning code restrictions

Necessary permits and licenses for operation

Laws and codes regarding zoning

Deed or lease restrictions such as covenants and restrictive conditions of purchase

Parking and customer access; deliveries

Sanitation, traffic and noise codes

Signs and advertising

Code requirements for space, ventilation, heat and

light

Limitations on the number and types of workers If not, check with the local Chamber of Commerce office

Reservations that neighbors may have about a business next to or near them

Is the Home Based Business Site Insurable?

In addition to community investigations, contact your insurance company or agent. It is almost certain that significant changes will be required in your coverage and limits when you start a home based business. When you have written a good description of your business, call your agent for help in insuring you properly against new hazards resulting from your business operations such as:

fire, theft and casualty damage to inventories and equipment

business interruption coverage

fidelity bonds for employees

liability for customers, vendors and others visiting the business workmen's compensation

group health and life insurance

product liability coverage if you make and/or sell a product; workmanship liability for services

business use of vehicle coverage

Overall Home Site Evaluation

After you have gathered as much information as seems practical you may wish to evaluate a home based site vs. one or more other nearby locations. Here's a handy checklist. Using the "0" to "10" scale, grade these vital factors:

Factors To Consider Grades for each factor: Home / Other

1. Customer convenience _____ _____

2. Availability of merchandise or raw materials _____ _____

3. Nearby competition _____ _____

4. Transportation availability and rates _____ _____

5. Quality and quantity of employees available

_____ _____

6. Availability of parking facilities _____ _____

7. Adequacy of utilities (sewer water, power, gas)

_____ _____

8. Traffic flow _____ _____

9. Tax burden _____ _____

10. Quality of police and fire services _____

_____

11. Environmental factors _____ _____

12. Physical suitability of building _____ _____

13. Provision for future expansion _____ _____

14. Vendor delivery access _____ _____

15. Personal convenience _____ _____

16. Cost of operation _____ _____

17. Other factors including how big can you get without moving _____ _____

The greater the difference between the totals of the two columns, the clearer your decision should be. In the space below. write out what your decision and the reasons that support it.

Decision:

_____

Writing the Business Plan

Now that your research and plan development is nearing completion, it is time to move into action. If you are still in favor of going ahead, it is time to take several specific steps. The key one is to organize your dream scheme into a business plan.

What is it?

Is written by the home based business owner with outside help as needed

Is accurate and concise as a result of careful study

Explains how the business will function in the marketplace

Clearly depicts its operational characteristics

Details how it will be financed

Outlines how it will be managed

Is the management and financial "blueprint" for startup and profitable operation

Serves as a prospectus for potential investors and lenders

Why create it?

The process of putting the business plan together including the thought that you put in before writing it, forces you to take an objective, critical, unemotional look at your entire business proposal

The finished written plan is an operational tool which, when properly used, will help you manage your business and work toward its success

The completed business plan is a means for communicating your ideas to others and provides the basis for your financing your business

Who should write it?

The home based owner to the extent possible

Seek assistance in weak areas, such as:

accounting

insurance

capital requirements

operational forecasting

tax and legal requirements

When should a Business Plan be used?

To make crucial startup decisions

To reassure lenders or backers

To measure operational progress

To test planning assumptions

As a basis for adjusting forecasts

To anticipate ongoing capital and cash requirements

As the benchmark for good operational management

Proposed Outline For Home Based Business Plan

This outline is suggested for a small proprietorship or family business. Shape it to fit your unique needs.

Part I. - Business Organization

cover Page:

A. Business Name: _____

Street Address: _____

Mailing Address: _____

Telephone number: _____

Owner(s) Name(s): _____

Inside Pages:

B. Business Form: _____

(proprietorship, partnership, corporation)

Include copies of key subsidiary documents in an appendix. Remember even partnerships require written agreements of terms and conditions to avoid later conflicts, and to establish legal entities and equities. Corporations require charters, articles of incorporation and by-laws.

Part II. - Business Purpose and Function

In this section write an accurate yet, concise description of the business. Describe the business you plan to start in narrative form.

What is the principal activity? Be specific. Give product and/or service description(s):

retail sales?

manufacturing?

service?

other?

How will it be started?

a new startup

the expansion of an existing business

purchase of a going business

a franchise operation

actual or projected start up date

Why will it succeed? Promote your idea!

how and why this business will be successful.

what is unique about your business

what is its market "niche"

What is your experience in this business? If you have a current resume of your career include it in an appendix and reference it here. Otherwise write a narrative here and include a resume in the finished product. If you lack specific experience, detail how you plan to gain it, such as training, apprenticeship or working with partners who have experience.

The Marketing Plan

The marketing plan is the core of your business rationale. To develop a consistent sales growth a home based business person must become knowledgeable about the market. To demonstrate your understanding, this section of the home based business plan should seek to concisely answer several basic questions:

Who is your market?

Describe the profile of your typical customer

Age:

Male, female, both:

How many in family:

Annual Family Income:

Location:

Buying patterns:

Reason to buy from you:

Other:

Geographically describe your trading area: (i.e. county, state, national, etc.)

_____

Economically describe your trading area: (single family, average earnings, number of children, etc.)

_____

How large is the market?

Total units or dollars:

Growing: _____ Steady: _____
Decreasing: _____

If growing, annual growth:

_____

Who is your competition? No small business operates in a vacuum. Get to know and respect the competition. Target your marketing plans. Identify direct competitors (both in terms of geography and product lines), and those who are similar or marginally comparative. Begin by listing names, addresses and products or services. Detail briefly but concisely the following information concerning each of your competitors:

Who are the nearest ones?

How are their businesses similar or competitive to

yours?

Do you have a unique "niche"? Describe it.

How will your service or product be better or more salable than your competitors?

Are their businesses growing? Stable? Declining? Why?

What can be learned from observing their operations and/or talking to their present or former clients?

Will you have competitive advantages or disadvantages by operating from home? Be honest!

Remember your business can become more profitable by adopting the good competitive practices and by avoiding their errors.

To help you evaluate how successful your product or service will be. go down. the following list of standard characteristics (you may want to add more from your knowledge of your field) and make a candid evaluation of your competitive "edge" On a scale of "0" (theirs puts mine to shame) to 10 (mine puts their to shame) indicate the potential for you and a total score:

Feature

Price _____

Performance _____

Durability _____

Versatility _____

Speed/accuracy _____

Ease of operation or use _____

Ease of maintenance or repair _____

Ease or cost of installation _____

Size or weight or color _____

Appearance or styling or packaging _____

Total Points _____

A Total Points score of less than 60 indicates that you might reconsider the viability of your product or service and/or think about how you can improve it. Over 80 points indicates a clear competitive edge.

What percent of the market will you penetrate?

1. estimate the market in total units or dollars

2. estimate your planned volume

3. amount your volume will add to total market

4. subtract 3 from 2

Line 4 represents the amount of your planned volume that must be taken away from the competition.

What pricing and sales terms are you planning? The primary consideration in pricing a product or service is the value that it represents to the customer, If on the previous checklist of features, your product is truly ahead of the field, you can command a premium price. On the other hand, if it is a "me too" product, you may have to "buy" a share of the market to get your foothold and then try to move price up later. This is always risky and difficult. One rule will always hold: ultimately the market will set the price. If your selling price does not exceed your costs and expenses by the margin necessary to keep your business healthy you will fail. Know your competitors pricing policies. Send a friend to comparison shop. Is there discounting? Special sales? Price leaders? Make some "blind" phone calls. Detail your pricing policy:

What is your sales plan? Describe how you will sell, distribute and or service what you sell? Be specific. Below are outlined some common practices:

Direct sales by telephone or in person. The tremendous growth of individual sales representatives who sell by party bookings, door to door and through distribution of call back promotional campaigns suggests that careful research is required to be profitable.

Mail Order. Specialized markets for leisure time or unique products have grown as more two income families find less time to shop. Be aware of recent mail order legislation and regulation.

Franchising

a. You may decide to either buy into someone else's franchise as a franchisee or

b. Create your own franchise operation that sells rights to specific territories or product lines to others. Each will require further legal, financial, and marketing research.

Distributors. You may decide to work as a local or regional distributor for several different product lines.

Outline your sales plan below:

_____

What is your advertising plan? Each product or service will need its own advertising strategy as part of the total business marketing plan. Before developing an advertising campaign for your business plan, take time to review a few basic assumptions. By definition, advertising is any form of paid, non-personal promotion that communicates with a large number of potential customers at the same time. The purpose of advertising is to inform, persuade and remind customers about your company's products or services. Every advertising activity should have specific goals. Common examples are:

To bring in sales orders or contracts

To promote special events such as sales, business openings, new products

To bring in requests for estimates or for a sales representative to call

A special goal at the outset may be to use special media to establish yourself even before startup and to get potential customer "feedback"

- These might include one or more of the following:

Purchase and distribution of business cards to potential clients

Posting notices on free bulletin boards in area supermarkets or office complexes

A telephone survey of potential clients to alert them to your startup plans.

To assist in determining what types of advertising are appropriate and within company budget projections, it will be necessary to carefully review your customer profile.

From this review, establish a clear statement of advertising goals. Write down what you want your advertising to accomplish:

The next step will be to develop answers to the following crucial questions:

Q. What should be said about the business and how should it be stated?

A. _____

Q. What media should be used?

A. _____

 Q. How much can be afforded?

A. _____

 Q. How can the advertising program be implemented?

A. _____

 Q. How can its effectiveness be measured?

A. _____

The basic criteria for selecting specific types of media will include concise answers to the following:

Trading Area - Do you plan to serve or sell to an industrial market, a national market, a neighborhood or specialized market? Describe yours:

_____

Customer Type - What does your potential customer read or listen to? Where? How often? What image does the media you are considering suggest? Does it fit your customer? Describe your customer:

_____

Budget Restrictions - How will the amount of money you have to spend limit the media you can use? How can you spread your budget out over a year to give a repetitive, continuous message? While you may have to spend more at the start, a good ongoing guideline is that advertising should not exceed one or two percent of sales. Set forth how much you are willing to invest in advertising in the first year: _____

Break into months or quarters:

_____

Continuity of Message - How will the type of product or service, customer profile and seasonal buying patterns affect your choice of media and the frequency with which you advertise? Explain your message here:

_____

Past Performance - What is the track record for use of the medium you are considering for your type of business? What do your competitors use? What does your trade association suggest? Enter appropriate comments here:

_____

Management Plan

Who will do what? Be sure to include four basic sets of information:

State a personal history of principals and related work, hobby or volunteer experience (include formal resumes in Appendix).

List and describe specific duties and responsibilities of each.

List benefits and other forms of compensation for each.

Identify other professional resources available to the business: Example: Accountant, lawyer, insurance broker, banker, etc. Describe relationship of each to business: Example: "accountant available on part time hourly basis, as needed, initial agreement calls for services not to exceed x hours per month at $ xx.xx per hour".

To make this section graphically clear, start with a

simple organizational chart that lists specific tasks and shows, who (type of person is more important than individual name) other than for principals will do what indicated by arrows, work flow and lines of responsibility and/or communications.

Concisely answer the following questions:

Q. What are your personnel needs now?

A: _____

Q. What skills must each key person have?

A: _____

Q. Are the people needed available? Name them, indicate full or part time and salary rates:

A: _____

Detail a proposed work schedule by week, and month for at least the first year.

If you have identified any gaps in personnel skills, state how these will be overcome by training, purchase of outside services, or subcontracting. Check with the nearest state employment service office for assistance. Write your plan:

_____

What is your banking plan?

What will be the location and type of bank accounts opened for the business. A word of caution, keep business accounts separate from personal or family accounts. These vital records will be necessary for future tax and accounting purposes. Describe your banking plan:

_____

How Is Your Credit Rating?

There may be several partial answers to this question. All will be of importance to the future of the business. First, what is your personal history of paying debts?

To establish a credit rating, it is necessary to secure credit with a number of businesses and to use it. Your rating will be based upon your record for paying for goods and services based upon the agreed terms. If your prior credit rating is poor discuss with your lawyer accountant and banker options for improvement before seeking and being refused business credit.

Operational Plans Summary

The purpose of this section is to summarize from previous sections, the various operations of your business and link them to the finance section of your business plan. In addition you will want to summarize the advantages and disadvantages of a home based business operation. Refer to your earlier checklist. Write your summary here:

The Financial Plan

Clearly the most critical section of your Business Plan Document is the Financial Plan. In formulating this part of the planning document, you will establish vital schedules that will guide the financial health of your business through the troubled waters of the first year and beyond.

Before going into the details of building the Financial Plan, it is important to realize that some basic knowledge of accounting is essential to the productive management of your business. If you are like most home business owners, you probably have a deep and abiding interest in the product or services that you sell or intend to sell. You like to do what you do, and it is even more fulfilling that you are making money doing it. There is nothing wrong with that. Your conviction that what you are doing or making is worthwhile is vitally important to success. Nonetheless, the income of a coach who takes the greatest pride in producing a winning team will largely depend on someone keeping score of the wins and losses.

The business owner is no different. Your product or service may improve the condition of mankind for generations to come, but, unless you have access to an unlimited bank roll, you will fail if you don't make a profit. If you don't know what's going on in your business, you are not in a very good position to assure its profitability. Most home based businesses will use the "cash" method of accounting with a system of recordkeeping that may be little more than a carefully annotated checkbook in which is recorded all receipts and all expenditures, backed up by a few forms of original entry (invoices, receipts, cash tickets, etc.)

If your business is, or will be, larger than just a small supplement to family income, you will need a something more sophisticated. Stationery stores can provide you with several packaged small business accounting systems complete with simple journals and ledgers and detailed instructions in understandable language.

Should you feel that your accounting knowledge is so rudimentary that you will need professional assistance to establish your accounting system, the classified section of your telephone directory can lead you to a number of small business services that offer a complete range of accounting services. You can buy as much as you need, from a simple "peg-board" system all the way to computerized accounting, and monthly profitability consultation. Rates are reasonable for the services rendered and an investigative consultation will usually be free. Look under the heading, "Business Consultants", and make some calls. Be sure to let them know the size of your business so you get to the ones who specialize in home based operations. Many of them are home-based entrepreneurs themselves and know what you will be going through.

Let's start by looking at the makeup of the Financial Plan for the business.

The Financial Plan includes the following:

1. Financial Planning Assumptions - these are

short statements of the conditions under which you plan to operate.

Market health:

Date of startup:

Sales buildup ($):

Gross profit margin:

Equipment, furniture and fixtures required:

Payroll and other key expenses that will impact the financial plan:

2. Operational Plan - Profit and Loss Projection - this is prepared for the first year broken into twelve individual months. It should become your first year's Budget.

3. Source of Funds Schedule - this shows the source(s) of your funds to capitalize the business and how they will be distributed among your fixed assets and working capital.

4. Pro Forma Balance Sheet - "Pro forma" refers to the fact that the balance sheet is before the fact, not actual. This form displays Assets, Liabilities and Equity of the business. This will indicate how much

Investment will be required by the business and how much of it will be used as Working Capital in its operation.

5. Cash Flow Projection - this will forecast the flow of cash into and out of your business through the year, It helps you plan for staged purchasing, high volume months and slow periods.

Creating the Profit and Loss Projection

Use the form below to create your own Profit and Loss Projection

Profit and Loss Projection

	Jan	Feb	Mar	Apr	May	Jun	Jul	Aug	Sep	Oct	Nov	Dec	Total
Sales													
(-) Cost of sales													
(=) Gross profit													
Controllable expenses													
Operating supplies													
Gross wages													
Repairs and maintenance													
Advertising													
Car and delivery													
Bad debts													
Administrative and legal													
Outside labor													
Miscellaneous expenses													
Total controllable exp													
Fixed expenses													
Rent													
Utilities													
Insurance													
Taxes and licenses													
Interest													
Depreciation													
Total fixed expenses													
Total expenses													
Net profit													

Source of Funds Schedule

To create this schedule, you will need to create a list of all of the Assets that you intend to use in your business, how much investment each will require and the source of funds to capitalize them.

Before you leave your Source of Funds Schedule, indicate the number of months (years x 12) of useful life for depreciable fixed assets. (In the example, the pickup truck, the packaging machine and the furniture and office equipment would be depreciable.)

You will need this data to enter as monthly depreciation on your Profit and Loss Projection. All of the data on the Source of Funds Schedule will be needed to create the Balance Sheet.

Creating the Pro Forma Balance Sheet

Here is a Balance Sheet form. There are a number of variations of this form and you may find it prudent to ask your banker for the form that the bank uses for small business. It will make it easier for them to evaluate the health of your business.

Even though you may plan to stags the purchase of some assets through the year for the purposes of this pro forma Balance Sheet, assume that all assets will be provided at the startup.

Cash Flow Projection

An important subsidiary schedule to your financial plan is a monthly Cash Flow Projection. Prudent business management practice is to keep no more cash in the business than is needed to operate it and to protect it from catastrophe. In most small businesses, the problem is rarely one of having too much cash. A Cash Flow Projection is made to advise management of the amount of cash that is going to be absorbed by the operation of the business and compares it against the amount that will be available.

Is Additional Money needed?

Suppose at this point you have determined that your business plan needs more money than can be generated by sales. What do you do?

What you do depends on the situation. For example, the need may be for bank credit to tide your business over during the lean months. This loan can be repaid during the fat sales months when expenses are far less than sales. Adequate working capital is necessary for success and survival.

A Final Word

In completing this worksheet, you have put in a great deal of time and effort. You should now have all of the elements needed to present as simple or sophisticated a prospectus for your enterprise as you desire. More important, you have created the management tools to guide you in your venture. Once the business opens its doors, you will be inundated by the details, problems, challenges and joys of going it alone. It will be difficult to hold to your course through the rough seas ahead, but don't forget this "chartbook", it will see you through to "Port Profit" It should be a living document, referred to regularly massaged constantly and revised to reflect your experience.

Begin a planning cycle that expands this first year plan into one that spans three or five years out. Update it at regular intervals. Set your goals and live by them. Your success is in your hands. Good planning and good execution!

9. Home Business Financial Planning

Begin your financial planning by estimating your initial or start-up costs. Include all items of a nonrecurring nature such as fees, licenses, permits, franchise fees, insurance, telephone deposit, tools, equipment, office supplies, fixtures, installation of fixtures and equipment, remodeling and decorating, funds for your opening promotional event if you plan to have one, signs, and, of course, professional fees for your attorney and accountant.

Depending on your type of operation, the amount of money you invest, and the energy you expect to put in (part-time to full-time) can determine how much working capital you will need. Many business experts say if you expect profit in six months, double that time and be ready to operate without profits for twelve months to give yourself a cushion in case of unanticipated expenses or delays. Study the growth patterns of other similar business and ask for advice from your accountant and attorney.

Projecting Operating Income and Expenses

Next, estimate the "working" capital you will need to keep operating for six to twelve months. Operating expenses include salaries; expenses for telephone, light, heat, office supplies, and other supplies or materials; debt interest; advertising fees;

maintenance costs; taxes; legal and accounting fees; insurance fees; business membership fees; and special services expenses, such as secretarial, copying, and delivery service.

It is a good idea to obtain typical operating ratios for the kind of business in which you are interested. Among the sources for such ratios are Robert Morris Associates, Dun & Bradstreet, Inc., the Accounting Corporation of America, trade associations, publishers of trade magazines, specialized accounting firms, industrial companies (for example, National Cash Register Co.), and colleges and universities. The typical ratios for your type of business combined with your estimated sales volume will serve as benchmarks for estimating the various items of expense. However, do not rely exclusively on this method for estimating each expense item. Modify these estimates through investigation and quotations in the particular market area where you plan to operate.

In addition to business operating capital, you will need to plan for reserve capital to cover personal expenses. This estimate will include all your normal living expenses, such as food, household expenses, car payments, rent or mortgage, clothing, medical expenses, entertainment, and taxes for you and your family.

After you have estimated start-up costs, working or operating capital needed for six to twelve months, and personal expenses and obligations, you may see that you need more start-up capital than you thought. What will you do? Discuss this with your accountant, attorney, and trusted business associates and family. Entrepreneurs secure needed capital in a variety of ways. You can:

* Get loans or gifts from family members or friends. Make businesslike, written agreements and be sure to disclose fully the potential risk as well as the possible profit.

* Apply for a bank loan. For this you will need a comprehensive statement of your personal financial condition and a business plan with financial projections to present to the loan officer. If you need help in preparing your loan application, take a course for small business people at a local community college or visit your nearest SBA office to get assistance from a SCORE counselor.

* Apply for an SBA loan guarantee. The SBA is not a bank, but it does extend guarantees and may rarely participate in a loan when the bank is unable or unwilling to provide the entire financing itself. The SBA loan officer will ask you the same hard questions as a loan officer in a commercial bank

and require the same carefully considered data on your personal finances, start-up costs, and business projections.

* Search for some sort of venture capital. For start-up entrepreneurs some prior managerial or entrepreneurial track record is usually necessary in order to get venture capital. The main disadvantage of venture capital is that you will probably have to give up between 50 to 90 percent ownership of the new business in return for the capital. A home business is extremely unlikely to attract venture capital.

Understanding Your Balance Sheet

Your Balance Sheet is a summary of the status of your business--i.e.., its assets, liabilities, and net worth--at an instant in time. By reviewing your Balance Sheet along with the Profit and Loss Statement and Cash-Flow Statement, you will be able to make informed financial and business planning decision.

The Balance Sheet is drawn up using the totals from the individual accounts kept in your General Ledger. It shows what you have left when you pay all your creditors. Assets less liabilities equal capital or net worth. The assets and liabilities sections must balance--hence the name Balance Sheet. It can be produced quarterly, semi-annually, or at the end of each calendar or fiscal year.

While your accountant will be most helpful in drawing up your Balance Sheet, it is you who must understand it. Current assets are anything of value you own such as cash, inventory, or property that the business owner can convert into cash within a year; fixed assets are things such as land and equipment. Liabilities are debts the business must pay. They may be current (such as amounts owed to suppliers or your accountant) or they may be long-term (such as notes owed to the bank). Capital (also called equity or net worth) is the excess of your assets over your liabilities.

Prepare a Balance Sheet for your new business during the planning phase to estimate its financial condition at that time and also a projected one for the first year of business. This will help you decide on the feasibility of your venture and make modifications to ensure profitability. You can also use these statements as part of the documentation in a loan application.

Understanding Your Profit and Loss Statement

Your Profit and Loss Statement is a detailed, month-by-month tally of the income from sales and the expenses incurred to generate the sales. It is a good assessment tool because it shows the effect of your decision on profit. It is a good planning tool because you can "try out" decisions on paper before actually going ahead.

The Profit and Loss Statement includes four kinds of information:

* The Sales information lists the number of units sold and the total revenues generated by the sales.

* The Direct Expenses category includes the cost of labor, materials, and manufacturing overhead (but not normal overhead).

* Indirect Expenses are the costs you have even if the product is not produced or the service is not delivered. They include the fixed costs or normal overhead of salaries, rent, utilities, insurance, depreciation, office supplies, taxes, and professional fees for your lawyers and accountant.

* Income or Profit is the last category on the Profit and Loss Statement. It is shown both as pre-tax and after-tax or net income. The IRS will look at your pre-tax figure, whereas your loan officer and you are more concerned with your after-tax figure.

Your Profit and Loss Statement should be prepared at the very minimum once a year--and more often in the beginning or growth stages of your business. It is a key document from which the economic health of a business can be determined. Make certain you do it properly and understand its meaning.

Understanding Your Cash Flow Statement

Your business must have a healthy cash flow to survive. Cash flow is the amount of money available in your business at any given time. To keep tabs on cash flow, forecast the funds you expect to disburse and receive over a given period of time. Then you can predict deficiencies or surplus in cash and decide how to respond.

A cash flow projection serves one other very useful purpose in addition to planning. As the actual information becomes available to you, compare it to the monthly cash flow estimates you previously made to see how accurately you are estimating. As you do this, you will be giving your self on-the-spot business training in making more accurate estimates and plans for the coming months. As your ability to estimate improves, your financial control of the business will increase.

The creative business owner works with his or her accountant to use the information gleaned from all of these financial tools to make a variety of managerial decisions--decisions on buying supplies, expansion, when to hire more employees, how to get the best tax breaks, and many other important steps that will shape the future of the business.

10. Record Keeping, Taxes, Insurance and Permits

Keeping accurate and up-to-date business records is, for many people, the most difficult and uninteresting aspect of operating a home-based business. If this area of business management is one that you anticipate will be hard for you, plan now how you will cope. Don't wait until tax time or until you are totally confused. Take a course at the local community college, ask a volunteer SCORE (Service Corps of Retired Executives) representative from the Small Business Administration to help you in the beginning, or hire an accountant to advise you on setting up and maintaining a recordkeeping system.

Your records will be used to prepare tax returns, make business decisions, and apply for loans. Set aside a special time each day to update your records. It will pay off in the long run with more deductions and fewer headaches.

If your business is small or related to an activity that is usually considered a hobby, it's even more important that you keep good records. The IRS may decide that what you are doing is only a hobby, and you won't be allowed to deduct expenses or losses from your home-produced income at tax time. So keep records of all transactions in which you spend or bring in money. Pick a name for your business and register it with local or state regulatory authorities. Call your city hall or county courthouse to find out how.

Your records should tell you these three facts:

* How much cash you owe,
* How much cash you are due, and
* How much cash you have on hand.

You should keep five basic journals:

1. Check register--Shows each check disbursed, the date of disbursement, number of the check, to whom it was made out (payee), the amount of money disbursed, and for what purpose.

2. Cash receipts--Shows the amount of money received, from whom, and for what.

3. Sales journal--Shows the business transaction, date, for whom it was performed, the amount of the invoice, and the sales tax, if applicable. it may be divided to indicate labor and goods.

4. Voucher register--A record of bills, money owed, the date of the bill, to whom it is owed, the amount, and the service.

5. General journal--A means of adjusting some entries in the other four journals.

Choosing a Recordkeeping System

Even though you may be small and just beginning, it is probably wise to consult an accountant to help you decide which recordkeeping system is best for your business. Once it is set up, you can record the daily transactions or periodically have a bookkeeper post your daily transactions in your General Ledger and prepare your financial statements.

Be sure to establish a separate bank account for your business--even before the first sale. Then you will have a complete and distinct record of your income and expenditures for tax purposes, and you won't have to remember which expenses were business and which were personal.

It is important to choose a recordkeeping system that you understand and will use. It will help you see how well the business is doing and is the first step in responsible financial management.

Tax Obligations And Benefits

Significant tax savings are available to the home-based businessowner in the form of deductions, credits, and depreciation allowances. The time, money, and energy you put into keeping good records and keeping current on tax laws will be worthwhile and ensure that you operate within the law. You will need to plan for income tax, social security (all self-employed persons must pay a federal self-employment tax), employees' taxes (if you hire anyone), property tax on your home and business-related taxes, such as sales tax, gross-receipts or inventory tax (in some states and localities), and excise or individual item taxes (on certain commodities).

The Internal Revenue Service supplies the following free booklets (and runs free workshops) to give you details on your specific obligations:

* Your Federal Income Tax (Publication 17)
* Tax Guide for Small Business (Publication 334)
* Business Use of Your Home (Publication 587)
* Employer's Tax Guide (Circular E)
* Self-Employment Tax (Publication 533)
* Tax Information on Retirement Plans for the Self-Employed (Publication 560)
* Tax Information on Depreciation (Publication 534)
* Information on Excise Taxes (Publication 510)

* Tax Withholding and Estimated Tax (Publication 505)

There are various federal and state forms you will need to fill out to start a small business. The federal government requires you to fill out several forms including the following:

* Application for Employer Identification Number (Form SS-4) (If you have employees or are subject to excise tax)
* Employer's Annual Unemployment Tax Return (Form 940)
* Employer's Quarterly Federal Tax Return (Form 941)
* Employee's Withholding Allowance Certificate (W-4)
* Employer's Wage and Tax Statement (W-2)
* Reconciliation/Transmittal of Income and Tax Statements (W-3)

As a home-based business owner you should be aware that every business decision--each purchase and transaction you make--has tax implications or built-in tax advantages or disadvantages.

Deductions may be available for home maintenance and improvements; automobile expenses; telephone expenses; office and work space; inventory space; major purchases, such as a computer; and a wide variety of other items such as uniforms, coffee service, trademarks, a safe deposit box, credit bureau fees, and business cards.

Each business situation is different and tax laws change, so consult up-to-date references, a trusted attorney, and an accountant who can advise you on your particular obligations and benefits.

Insurance

Insurance helps to safeguard your business against losses from fire, illness, and injury. You cannot operate without it. Talk with an insurance representative about your business needs. Check with the insurance carriers on your home policy and make sure business use of your home is compatible with your homeowner's policy. In addition to a homeowner's policy (personal plan), now that you have a business, you will need a commercial policy for full protection. Discuss these other possible needs with your agent:

* Product Liability Coverage--to protect you in case your product causes injury to the user

* Auto Liability and "Non-owned" Auto Liability Insurance--if a car is ever used to support the business in any way

* Medical Payments Insurance--payable if someone is injured in your home whether or not it was your fault

* Worker's Compensation--if you have employees

* Business Interruption Insurance or Earnings Insurance--in case your business is damaged by fire or some other cause and you must totally or partially suspend operations
* Disability Income Protection--a form of health insurance in case you become disabled

* Business Life Insurance--to provide funds for transition if you die

Be sure to keep all your insurance records and policies in a safe place--either with your accountant or in a safe deposit box. If you keep them at home for convenience sake, then give your policy numbers and insurance company names to your accountant or lawyer or put it in your safe deposit box.

Final advice for the wise business person is to read and understand the fine print in all policies and to reevaluate business insurance needs about every six months.

Other Considerations

Another aspect of planning is sheltering tax dollars through a Keogh Plan or corporate pension and profit-sharing plans, if your business is incorporated, or a retirement plan.

If you have a partnership, consider making a Buy and Sell Agreement with your partner(s). This agreement requires the surviving partner(s) to buy, and the heirs to sell, the deceased partner's interest. The surviving partner(s) then becomes the sole owner(s) and the heirs receive cash for their share of the business.

Dealing With Laws: Zoning, Licensing, Permits, and Others

Unfortunately, many home-based business people try to "slide" into business, saying "I'll just try it for a few months and see how things go" or "It's not really a business. I have only ten clients." This attitude can lead to a lack of planning and big disappointments. If you set up your studio, print business cards and flyers announcing classes, and then find that regulations make it illegal to operate out of your home, you may have to start all over.

Zoning

Before you start your home-based business, do a thorough investigation of the zoning laws in your community. Zoning regulations spell out activities permitted and prohibited in specific portions of a city or county. Call your town hall, zoning office, or local library to get a copy of zoning laws. Find out the structure of your local zoning groups. Most areas have Planning, Zoning, and Appeals Boards.

If the home business you are planning conforms to zoning regulations, then all you need to do is keep abreast of new proposals that may affect your situation. It's a good idea to stay in touch with others operating from their homes by joining business organizations or neighborhood groups in case you ever need to band together to propose or oppose new regulations. Maintaining a low profile and friendly relations with your neighbors will result in more support from them should adverse regulations affecting your business ever be proposed.

If through your research you discover that the home business you are planning would violate the zoning code, there are several possible ways to proceed. You might wish to check with an attorney who specializes in zoning law to look for a legal way around the regulation. You might decide to apply to the Zoning Board for a variance or exception. Or you may be able to change your business enough to make the operation fit the law. If the regulation outlaws businesses that employ people other than the owner at home, maybe you can have employees take work to their own homes. If your business will create too much traffic, consider another strategy for product distribution. If your business will create too much noise, maybe you can soundproof your house. At last resort, ask yourself "Is it worth it to organize a drive to change the law?" Considering the rapid growth in the number of home-based businesses, you just might find other entrepreneurs who are also interested in submitting a change in the regulations to the Zoning Board. Go to meetings of the Board and try to identify the person who appears most active and most sympathetic to your position.

In the unfortunate and unlikely (most zoning officers don't have time to chase people who aren't bothering anybody) event that you are issued a "cease and desist" order, you should: 1) file an appeal immediately with the Appeals Board (if you interpret the regulations differently than they do); or 2) submit a change in the regulation to the Zoning Board to allow your business, which may enable you to continue to operate without fines until the Board reaches a decision. You may need a lawyer if you are not entirely familiar with the regulations and the workings of the Board.

Cultural and national trends point in the direction of zoning regulations that allow quiet, nonpolluting, low-traffic kinds of home businesses. More and more corporations are employing people to work at home. Most neighborhoods will adopt a "live and let live" attitude if you keep your premises neat and quiet and don't create traffic and parking problems.

Keeping Up With Zoning Legislation

There are two ways to keep up with zoning legislation in your community (and with other topics of interest to home-based entrepreneurs). One way is to read local newspapers, especially the business section and the local or "neighborhood" sections. Be sure you notice local items about such things as proposed subway stations or the county's plan for revitalization. Changes like these could eventually influence zoning in your area. The other way to keep abreast of trends and zoning issues is to join the local chapter of a business group, such as the Rotary Club, the National Association of Women Business Owners, the National Family Business Council, or a Business and Professional Women's Club. Through newsletters, meetings, and friendships that develop, you will hear all the latest local (and national) issues discussed while you learn valuable business skills and make useful contacts.

11. How to Build a Favorable Image of Your Business

Introducing a new, home-based service business into a local competitive market requires a clear understanding of how the unique characteristics of a home based service business and the consumer decision making process (buyer-readiness stages) affect the initial promotion mix decision. This paper concludes with a practical discussion of appropriate promotion ideas for new, home-based service businesses.

Currently, more than millions of business owners operate full-time businesses from their homes. In addition, another millions operate part-time home-based businesses. Not only can having a home-based business reduce operating expenses, it also offers one the opportunity to work at his or her own pace and hours.

But despite their growing popularity, home-based business people are, in some instances, not taken seriously. The impression held is that a home-based business person is only playing at being in business. This can be especially true of new, home-based service businesses; their lack of a tangible product makes them vulnerable to questions concerning their quality. In fact, competitors can take advantage of this aspect by adopting a competitive strategy that portrays the home-based business as lacking in experience and stability.

The purpose of this guide is to describe the ways in which a new, home-based service business is unique and propose ways in which such a business can effectively position itself among competitors who are serving the same local market. In particular, this paper deals with home-based businesses in which there is no face-to-face customer contact within the home. And because promotional strategies emphasizing purchase are fruitless unless the consumer is cognizant of the service, this paper will further focus on the initial buyer-readiness states of awareness and knowledge.

Understanding The Nature Of A Home Based Service Business

There are typically four characteristics associated with a business that provides a service: intangibility, inseparability, and variability, and perishability. Each of these characteristics are also true of a home-based service business. But the first two traits, intangibility and inseparability, seem to create particular problems for the home-based service business.

The characteristic of intangibility implies that it is impossible for a customer to see or touch what the service business has to offer. Therefore, it is generally difficult to know prior to purchase the quality of the service. This difficulty is compounded for the home-based service business if the business does not offer a physical location in which to interact with a customer. Even those owners who want to provide space for customer interaction are often stymied by zoning laws. Yet in non-home-based businesses, aspects of a company's physical location are often used as substitutes for a tangible product: The face of the building, the signage, and the interior decor are all capable of subtly telling a customer that a business is stable, reliable, and professional. Many home-based businesses do not have this opportunity.

The second difficulty that a home-based service business faces is related to the trait of inseparability: It is commonly suggested that the service provided by a business cannot be separated from the person who provides it. (4) This implies that the visibility of the service provider is key to the success of the business. So without a physical location within the business community, the home-based business person even lacks the daily opportunities for personal interaction--the visibility--that simply going to and leaving from a non-home-based business would provide.

Focusing On The Proper Promotion Mix

To overcome the difficulties inherent in being a home-based service business, one must carefully analyze the opportunities for counteracting these difficulties in each stage of the consumer decision making process. The Hierarchy-of-Effects Model suggests that the stages through which a consumer passes are awareness, knowledge, liking, preference, conviction, and purchase. Of particular importance to this discussion are the initial stages of the process in which the owner of a new, home-based service business must seek a cognitive response from the potential consumer. In a study by Wilson and Hainault, it was found that non-users of a service had lower perceptions of quality than did users. Therefore, image characteristics must be conveyed to the target market early in the decision process. The business must design a promotion strategy that creates visibility and communicates clearly the traits of experience, reliability, and professionalism so as to move the target audience through those initial buyer-readiness stages of awareness and knowledge.

Communicating to potential customers can be done through the use of several promotion tools: advertising, personal selling, sales promotion, and public relations. Selecting the proper promotion mix--the combination of tools to be used--requires a matching between the stage of buyer-readiness and the tool or tools most appropriate for that stage. According to Kotler in Marketing Management, advertising and public relations are the tools considered most effective in the early stages of buyer-readiness. (4)

The Initial Promotion Strategy For The New, Home Based Service Business

What does this mean then for the new, home-based service business? Consider, for example, a carpet cleaning service. A strategy that begins with a sales promotion tool such as a coupon may have less than the desired results. Certainly there will be some responses from price sensitive consumers. But the target market as a whole will not react because they have no knowledge of the company; the business has no image that will portray to potential customers the company's experience at carpet cleaning, its reliability, or the quality of its work.

To demonstrate how the selection of the promotion mix should be applied to create the appropriate image for a new, home-based business, three home-based scenarios have been developed--a furniture re-upholsterer, an accountant, and a house and pet sitter. Each example will (1) focus on counteracting the difficulties that stem from the service characteristics, intangibility and inseparability, and demonstrate the use of advertising and public relations as methods for moving the target audience through the awareness and knowledge stages of buyer-readiness.

Furniture Re-upholsterer

A furniture re-upholsterer has the opportunity to create a substitute for a tangible product in the vehicle he or she drives. While a new vehicle certainly seems to say "prosperous," every home-based business owner cannot afford to purchase a new vehicle. A used vehicle can be an effective tool if it is clean (inside and outside) and if it has professional signage displaying the company's logo, name, and phone number. In a sense, the vehicle takes the place of the office and furnishings of a non-home-based business.

In addition, a furniture re-upholsterer should pay attention to personal dress and grooming as the appearance of the re-upholsterer conveys a strong message to the potential buyer. In his Model of Service Perceptions, Gronroos points out that functional quality (attitudes, behaviors, appearances) has an impact on a company's image just as technical expertise or quality does. A uniform or clean work clothes, then, can speak volumes about the care a re-upholsterer will give someone's furniture. Of course we all know someone who is really good at what he or she does, but the person's grooming and dress habits don't reflect that expertise. Poor appearance can be overcome, but it takes time; it takes considerable word of mouth about one's abilities to overcome one's idiosyncrasies. Why waste that time in getting the business off the ground?

Other ways to generate awareness and knowledge include the following: One possibility is to rent space at a home and garden show. The business owner could reupholster an item throughout the duration of the show and give advice freely to questions asked. The re-upholsterer will have gained visibility, created a substitute tangible product (the item being reupholstered), and promoted his or her level of expertise.

A second possibility is to offer to teach a continuing education class in reupholstering at the local community college. In general, "teacher = expert" in the minds of consumers. Students in the class become potential customers for more difficult reupholstering jobs they might have; and word-of-mouth referrals from the students are also likely to occur.

A third idea for establishing the image of a new, home-based re-upholsterer would be to contact an established antique dealer and offer to reupholster something in return for referrals or the opportunity to display business cards at the dealer's shop. This possibility is especially important because it puts knowledge of the re-upholsterer's abilities in the hands of an opinion leader, someone from whom others might seek advice.

Accountant

A new, home-based accountant has even more difficulty demonstrating the quality of his or her work than does the re-upholsterer. A finished chair can always be shown to a potential customer. But what can an accountant show? Creating an image of tangible quality is much more difficult.

So the accountant must focus on the things that represent the service provided. That means a well-designed logo that appears on quality stationery, business cards, and brochures. (These items are important to all three of the service businesses discussed herein, but are particularly important to the accountant.) The accountant must also focus on the characteristic of inseparability and recognize that his or her every move reflects upon the business.

Potential ideas for creating awareness and knowledge in the target audience are as follows: The accountant could use the repetition that advertising provides by placing a multiple-time ad in the newspaper. The ad should announce the opening of the business and stress the experience, training, and specialty of the owner. A picture of the accountant will help the target audience attach a visual image to the company name. The accountant should not expect instant phone calls as this ad is strictly for building awareness.

To emphasize the experience of the accountant, he or she could undertake a variety of activities: offer to write a column for the local Chamber of Commerce newsletter; offer to give free lectures or seminars to Chamber or other civic organization groups; and submit a news release for the newspaper's Business or Personnel Update column that indicates recent continuing education course work or seminars taken.

To initiate word-of-mouth communication about the quality of the his or her work, the accountant could donate his or her services to a highly visible nonprofit organization.

House and Pet Sitter

A firm foundation of trust is required to allow a stranger into one's house when no one is at home. This trust can be built from two perspectives:

opportunities for personal interaction and comments spread word-of-mouth by opinion leaders. So a newly established house and pet sitter would want to look for opportunities to display his or her trustworthiness to potential customers in whatever arena possible. This might mean doing volunteer work with a nonprofit organization, working on Chamber committees, etc. Responsibility displayed in one situation leaves the impression that one will be responsible in other situations.

One way to initiate word-of-mouth communications is for the sitter to donate his or her services to a fund-raising auction such as one held for a public television station. This allows not only awareness exposure during the auction but also a chance to demonstrate the quality of the services provided.

The house and pet sitter might also use the technique Pike calls "farming." A take-off on segmenting, farming involves concentrating on a specific neighborhood. The sitter could go door-to-door introducing himself or herself and handing out flyers. In addition, the sitter could stage a cutest and ugliest dog contest in a nearby park where his or her image as a person who likes and gets along well with animals is clearly exhibited. Both the door-to-door activity and the dog contest give the sitter opportunities for personal, trust-building interaction with the target audience.

Conclusion

The foregoing discussion centered upon the initial promotion strategy that is necessary for a new, home-based service business to undertake to begin building its image. Obviously, the promotion strategy cannot stop there. Additional uses of the promotional tools must be added to the promotion mix as some members of the target audience move past the awareness and knowledge stages. This means that the promotion mix will then include the use of tools that appeal to potential customers at all stages of the buyer- readiness process. The key issue, though, for a new, home based service business is recognizing the starting point. Creating a promotion mix that has appeal for consumers in all stages of the buyer-readiness means that money has been wasted on inappropriate techniques. The message is clear: The consumer goes through successive steps prior to making the decision to purchase. Focusing on the initial stages of the consumer decision making process lays the groundwork for the success of future promotional tools.

www.ingramcontent.com/pod-product-compliance
Lightning Source LLC
Chambersburg PA
CBHW072216170526
45158CB00002BA/621